Road to Heros Camp

Frank Anderson III

Road To Heroes Camp

Frank Anderson III

ISBN Number 979-8-89283 -164-2

This book would not have been possible without the unwavering support of Pat/Bj Magley, Patrick Perri and Kelly Magley Perri.

Contents

A heartfelt thank you to everyone who made this book possible.

Preface

This is a story about faith, love, and perseverance. It is about breaking barriers, overcoming adversity, and answering a higher calling.

At its core, this book is the testimony of two lives—Pat and BJ Magley—whose love for God and each other led to a mission that would touch the hearts and lives of countless young men.

In the 1970s, amidst racial tension and societal challenges, Pat and BJ's unlikely union sparked a journey that would stretch far beyond themselves. Pat's dream of the NBA may have been derailed, but it paved the way for a far greater purpose: the creation of Heroes Camp. Through prayer, sacrifice, and relentless faith, Heroes Camp became a beacon of hope for young men in need of guidance, love, and opportunity.

This book recounts their incredible story, from their beginnings as a couple facing unimaginable odds to their decades of selfless service. It's about finding purpose in the midst of disappointment, choosing faith over fear, and trusting that God's plan is always greater.

Preface

May this story inspire you to pursue your own calling with courage, to love without limits, and to believe that no matter the odds, miracles are always possible.

Frank Anderson III

ROAD TO HEROES CAMP

*HEROES ARE BORN, NOT MADE; THEY BLEED
EMOTIONALLY, MENTALLY, AND PHYSICALLY
TO BUILD THE ROAD FOR FUTURE HEROES*

Introduction

When we think of a "hero," we often picture someone with many skills, incredible powers, unique qualities, a charming personality, and countless achievements. Their successes fascinate and motivate us, making us dream about all they have accomplished. But we often overlook their struggles and hardships. We celebrate their victories but don't support them during their dark times. We praise their efforts and applaud their success but don't stand by them when they need us most. They are heroes because they did what they believed was right for themselves and society. They are ordinary people, but their journey is extraordinary. They carve the path to becoming heroes by shedding tears, facing criticism, and showing unwavering dedication and enthusiasm.

Though heroes have some inborn abilities that set them apart, those same traits can leave them feeling isolated when they choose an unusual path. This path is difficult and presents challenges at every step of their journey.

Have you ever wondered how a hero is formed? What sets them apart from others? Why are they considered heroes when many people do similar things? While they may have some natural instincts that keep their passion alive, many other factors shape them into the best version of themselves. The society they live in, the culture they reflect, and the mix of positive and negative influences around them push them to take an unusual path. They listen to their inner voice and use negative forces as motivation. They walk a path full of thorns and hardships, challenging common perceptions and societal norms to create new standards.

This story is about one of those heroes who was once an outcast. He saw life differently and went against societal norms because he believed it was the right thing to do. He loved deeply and fought bravely. His commitment to the woman he loved was so strong that he ignored what society thought of him. He faced obstacles from family, friends, and society with courage. He worked to eliminate racial antagonism in his community. He changed not only people's behavior but also the laws, showing us that nothing can stop us from loving someone and succeeding in life.

This story is about Pat and BJ Magley, who belong to different races, but whose love is so strong that they changed society's perceptions. Pat dreamed of playing in the NBA and had the talent to make it happen, but he sacrificed his dream because it meant leaving behind the girl he loved with all his heart. Pat and BJ came from different races, cultures, and societal backgrounds, and their circumstances were far from favorable. During the presidency of Richard Nixon, racial tension was high in America. Despite the discrimination, Pat Magley, a white man, fell in love with Bobbie Jean (BJ) Simmons, a black woman, while they were studying at West Georgia College in Carrollton, GA. Their love was so controversial that society and even their parents disapproved. Pat's dream of playing in the NBA was shattered, but something greater was destined for them.

Pat and BJ's love grew stronger with every hurdle they faced, ultimately leading to changes in laws and societal behavior. Pat truly demonstrated what it means to love as a gentleman.

Though Pat's choice to follow his heart cost him his dream of playing in the NBA, the couple found another way to fulfill their lives and help others facing similar challenges. They founded Heroes Camp, a place that guides those who, like Pat and BJ, choose the difficult path in life. They became torch-bearers, role models, and heroes for anyone who has ever loved and chosen a challenging road. They set an example that nothing can defeat you if you are determined and committed to your goal.

This book is a source of motivation for those who aspire to achieve great things but fear the challenges that might disrupt their journey. It offers lessons for those who feel unable to share their love due to social and cultural barriers. It reminds you that only you can defeat yourself; no one else has the power to stop you from pursuing your dreams.

Life is too short, and everyone deserves happiness and success. But success comes only if you are determined, like BJ and Pat. You may have surrendered some dreams, but you can still make them a reality in another way.

Every page of this book reveals how difficult it is to sacrifice everything for love, but in the end, you'll realize it's worth it when you achieve your goal. Read this book to make a fresh start and thrive in the areas of your choice. Embrace a rebirth and start from scratch. Remember, you can achieve what you want if you stay consistent and committed. Each page will boost your motivation and deepen your love for humanity.

Read to embrace a life of high motivation and freedom, and to serve humanity for the greater good.

Chapter 1

Young and Dumb

S ocial and mental evolution is shaped by society's influence on one's life. While society teaches valuable lessons, not all its teachings align with your personality and thoughts.

Certainly, every society has flaws that some notice from a young age, but only a few have the courage to speak out about these issues. Society may label these courageous individuals as outlaws, but they are the true heroes who can shift traditional mindsets. These heroes don't just criticize the system; they refuse to conform to it because it contradicts their inherent beliefs and principles. They are genuine catalysts for change, not merely participants in change.

Pat Magley is one of those heroes who did what was right for him and became a catalyst for historical and societal change. Unlike many, he didn't wait for the perfect moment or widespread support to act on his beliefs. Instead, he listened to his inner instincts and bravely chose the unconventional path, regardless of the consequences.

Pat Magley, a hero of humanity, was born to Bill and Mary Magley, who lived in an all-white neighborhood. His father, an orphan with a typical white mindset, worked as a factory worker and was a talented athlete. Pat, the eldest of four siblings—David, Susan, and Billy Magley—inherited his athletic genes from his father. His father played minor league baseball for the Chicago Cubs, was a middleweight champion in seven states, and served as an umpire chief for fast-pitch softball for 25 years. He even fought on the same ticket as Joe Louis. Pat's training in catching and handling a ball began at the early age of three or four, when his father played catch with him. By the age of six, he had a bat in his hand, and by seven, he was already playing basketball. Movement and sports have been a significant part of his life since childhood.

At that time, neither Bill nor Mary Magley knew that a future basketball pro and historical figure was growing up in their home. They lived in a typical Catholic household in a predominantly white neighborhood, sharing similar thoughts to many others in the USA. Tragically, Mary Magley, who passed away from cancer in 1977 at the age of 57, marked another chapter of grief and sadness for Pat. Pat's father, Bill Magley, died in 1999 at the age of 82. He went to the hospital with a broken hip, never recovered, and passed away shortly thereafter.

Pat was a highly sensitive child from early on. His thoughts and perceptions of society differed from those of his peers. He contemplated issues that were considered taboo for a white child during a time of severe racial discrimination in America. White people were generally unwilling to associate with Blacks, and any such interactions often faced hostile aggression. Pat grew up pondering the societal inequalities and the attitudes of whites toward Blacks. At that time, he didn't fully understand the implications of his thoughts on his own future and that of his family. An inner voice began to stir, expressing discontent with the deep societal divisions he observed.

He was young and inexperienced, seeking answers to questions that weren't fully clear to him. He struggled to find the right words to discuss racial disparities and was uncertain about whom he could confide in about these issues. Pat questioned why people were treated differently solely based on their skin color. He couldn't articulate his empathy towards Black individuals. Unaware of the societal norms, he didn't realize that his affinity for the Black community was considered a serious offense by many white Americans.

David Magley, Pat Magley's younger brother, remembers their childhood as challenging yet focused on sports. David describes Pat's unmatched passion for basketball, noting his resilience and love for the game. Pat's dedication inspired David to achieve the title of **"*Mr. Basketball*"** in Indiana, competing against 117 other cities in the state. Recalling one intense summer day in Indiana, David reminisces, "The sun was scorching, and Pat insisted on teaching me to catch and dunk the ball while running. My sneakers were melting on the hot asphalt, and I just wanted to go home." Despite David's initial reluctance, Pat's determination pushed him to stay on the court until he succeeded. David credits Pat not only for his tough coaching but also for transforming their community's perspective on basketball.

In high school, Pat noticed a prevailing negative attitude toward black people among his friends, teachers, and society at large. In his community, befriending or associating with black individuals was seen as unethical, unbearable, and unconventional. Pat struggled with whether this issue was localized or a broader global problem. However, his feelings found expression when **James Brown** sang *"Say It Loud – I'm Black and I'm Proud"* in 1968, often referred to as the "Black National Anthem." The lyrics deeply resonated with Pat, influencing not only him but also many others in their community. The song gave Pat a sense of purpose and inspired him to challenge societal norms, recognizing that, deep down, he shared common humanity with his black friends.

In the 1950s and 1960s, the idea of transition and interracial cooperation was unimaginable. This was the time when Pat, becoming increasingly aware, confronted racial issues on all fronts. His neighborhood was staunchly resistant to integration, presenting immense challenges. Despite this environment, Pat, a white teenager with a deep compassion for humanity, began forging friendships and playing basketball with black peers. He created lasting memories by joining them on different courts, visiting their homes, and sharing meals with their families. Pat's sensitivity allowed him to notice the negative reactions from people as he formed interracial connections with classmates and teammates. At just 14 years old, he witnessed firsthand the hardships faced by black people due to racial discrimination, encountering strong opposition to his social integration efforts.

Despite facing intense tension and widespread opposition in his neighborhood, Pat refused to bow to societal norms. Innately heroic, he remained steadfast in his belief that he was on the right path. Pat demonstrated his conviction by inviting friends, teammates, and peers from various high schools to join him in playing at his childhood playground—a larger, more expansive space in town with ample room for players.

In taking this initiative, Pat laid the foundation for significant historical change aimed at dismantling racial discrimination. His actions marked the beginning of a movement toward greater inclusivity and equality in his community.

The parking lot filled with nearly 50 cars as guys from Penn, Plymouth, and every high school in South Bend gathered to play. Despite the turnout, Pat's efforts at integration were met with strong opposition from his neighborhood. Slogans like *"**Niggas not welcome**"* were boldly written across his entire driveway. In a malicious act, someone even tried to harm him by cutting down a large tree in his backyard, which his mother attributed to a tornado. The neighborhood's hostility toward Pat intensified, fueled by the belief that beneath his charming and athletic exterior, there was a black man living within him.

He endured widespread hatred in the town but remained unwavering in his beliefs. Pat was deeply committed to his principles and dedicated to promoting interracial interaction. His family also bore the brunt of his convictions. Pat's parents received threatening letters and endured persistent gossip. Each morning brought new threats in their mailbox. Furthermore, Pat's younger sister faced harassment at school from boys who disapproved of her brother's friendships and support for black people.

Despite the relentless hostility from his neighborhood and school, everyone's efforts to discourage him only fueled Pat's determination. Unbeknownst to them, they were unwittingly shaping a hero. Pat used every threat and setback as motivation to deepen his bonds with his black friends and teammates. Instead of succumbing to opposition, he embraced it as a catalyst for personal growth. Each challenge strengthened his commitment to higher moral principles and heightened his empathy for humanity as a whole.

Indeed, Pat emerged as a humanitarian hero dedicated to eradicating racial discrimination from society. His efforts brought about a historical transformation in South Bend, Indiana. Pat became a symbol of unity, representing both black and white communities and embodying the ideals of equality and justice. His courage and commitment made a profound impact, resonating far beyond his local community.

The repercussions of Pat's interracial advocacy extended beyond himself to affect his siblings and parents, who faced hostility from their community and broader society. Pat's mother empathized with him, but she stood by his father, despite their differing views. Despite these challenges, Pat always gleaned valuable life lessons from his parents. He understood that their actions were not intended to harm him; rather, they were constrained by societal norms. Following in the footsteps of his parents' integrity and perseverance, Pat earned a scholarship to attend college, continuing to uphold their golden principles in his pursuit of education and social change.

The environment Pat faced in both school and college mirrored the discrimination prevalent in his neighborhood. Teachers and peers alike were influenced by racial prejudice, promoting white supremacy and condemning interracial relationships. Despite this pervasive opposition, Pat remained steadfast in his beliefs and actions. What set Pat apart was his innate rejection of racial inequality. He did not seek approval from his community or school; instead, he steadfastly pursued what he believed was just and ethical. From a young age, Pat held a strong conviction that skin color was merely an external trait, bearing no significance on human nature. He firmly believed that internally, all humans are fundamentally the

Young and Dumb

same. Pat's unwavering commitment to these principles shaped his path as a future hero, driven by his belief in equality and the inherent dignity of every individual.

Religion is often a refuge for many, but Pat had no such sanctuary. Standing tall at 6 feet 7 inches, he couldn't escape notice anywhere, even in church, where eyes followed him with curiosity. Despite his visibility, Pat didn't seek to avoid criticism or evade people's anger. Instead, he remained true to himself, steadfast in doing what he believed was right.

Success in life requires clear goals and the determination to overcome challenges in pursuit of your dreams. Athletics ran in Pat's family, but he aspired to achieve more than anyone else.

Pat's passion for basketball, supported by his childhood friend **Doug Willoughby**, is well-documented. Doug, who has known Pat since they were six years old, grew up alongside him in their neighborhood and attended school together. Their bond continued until Dough moved away at the age of 25. They spent countless hours at West Haven Park, playing various sports like baseball in spring, football in fall, and clearing snow from the basketball court in winter to play basketball. In summer, Pat would wake Doug up around 7 to 7:30 am by tapping on his bedroom window, eager to head to the court for a game before breakfast.

Pat's passion for basketball was infectious. His goal was to play in the NBA, and he worked tirelessly to earn a college scholarship, knowing it was the most direct path to realizing his dream. With his exceptional height and magical skills, he was a perfect fit for the NBA and gained widespread favor. Everything seemed aligned for Pat, except for the challenges posed by his thoughts and actions regarding race.

Pat was soaring in life, achieving great heights, unaware that racial injustice would shatter his dreams. He was a hard worker, a naturally talented athlete, and a kind-hearted person loved by all. Little did he know, God had a greater plan for him. His influential persona would challenge prejudiced beliefs and societal norms. Choosing humanity over personal ambition, he would become a beacon of change, breaking through decades-old barriers. If history teaches us anything, Pat's efforts and sacrifices will be remembered for centuries.

Pat was an ordinary man who loved playing basketball and spending time with friends. But circumstances turned him into a hero. His community strongly opposed his beliefs, leading to betrayal and hatred from friends and neighbors. Instead of letting this adversity deter him, Pat used it as motivation to forge his own path. His cause was noble, his views were unique, and he became a hero in every sense. He paved the way to Heroes Camp, where everyone could showcase their ideas and talents, ushering in a new era of freedom and hope. Despite facing loneliness and community opposition, Pat's self-confidence grew stronger. He remained steadfast in his convictions, undeterred by others' actions, and remained committed to what he believed was right.

Chapter 2

The Struggle to be Together

"Freedom is a struggle, and we do it together. Not only together as black citizens, but black and white together"- Andrew Young

L ife is like a race, and the harsh truth is that winners often surround themselves with other winners. If you're someone who struggles, especially if you go against societal norms, you'll encounter unprecedented challenges. These obstacles and setbacks can embitter you and sometimes lead you astray from your path. But heroes possess a different mindset from the majority. They listen to their inner voices and use obstacles as stepping stones toward their goals.

Despite Pat's challenges at home, in his neighborhood, school, and college, he couldn't foresee the bitterness awaiting him in the days ahead. His efforts towards interracial collaboration were about to enter a new era of pain and struggle. Little did he know that reaching the NBA would remain only a dream for him.

Pat's deep commitment to humanity and equality set him apart. He wasn't biased against white or exclusively supportive of black people; rather, he sought to bridge the divide between them. His mission was to combat racial discrimination, regardless of whether it stemmed from whites or blacks. He aimed to eradicate this societal evil. Despite not wanting to hurt his family, neighborhood, teachers, or others in society, he remained steadfast in his convictions. His conscience urged him to stand up for what was right and oppose injustice.

Pat's empathy and love across racial lines brought him trouble. In his stubborn neighborhood, showing affection for blacks was unacceptable. Coaches who should have supported him were racist, teaching biased ideas. Their goal was to exclude blacks, including Pat. Some black individuals also responded to racism with retaliation. The entire society seemed sick and suffocating for someone like Pat, who lived with a golden heart.

It was a time filled with frustration, agitation, screaming, and tears. Pat felt misunderstood by everyone—at home, at school, and on the basketball court. He loved his parents dearly, and they loved him, but his unconventional path was causing constant hurdles. His support for the black community sometimes made his father angry. Pat understood his parents were good people and not to blame, but he felt powerless because he was simply following what felt right to him.

Pat led a solitary life with little interest at home, trying to avoid his father and seeking understanding friends. He was full of energy and movement, unused to being alone, yet he couldn't relate to others' lives. During this time, basketball became his sole companion and outlet. Although a talented player, he used the game to clear his mind. It was during this period that Pat met some of the most important people in his life—his true friends who stood by him through all the hardships. They were his teammates, loyal friends, and companions during his darkest times.

Amidst his frustration and search for purpose, Pat's mother tragically passed away from cancer. She had always been a supportive and strong presence in his life, often defending him from his father. Her death marked a new period of anguish and turmoil for Pat. Meanwhile, his father remarried, leaving Pat to wander the streets in search of peace and happiness.

Pat was highly visible and well-known at every level due to his tall stature, athletic prowess, especially in basketball, which made him popular not only in his city but also in nearby towns. He desired recognition as a basketball pro or for something different, but unfortunately, people perceived him differently. They viewed him as a troublemaker, attributing chaos and unrest in South Bend, Indiana to him. They saw him as a white man who sided with the black community. Pat wanted to clarify that he wasn't a troublemaker but someone troubled by societal issues. He wasn't trying to harm anyone; rather, he stood for humanity, love, and equality. Despite this, no one seemed willing to understand him. He was even sent downtown for psychological analysis because many believed he identified as black despite his white appearance. Pat knew his racial identity was white but opposed the widespread racial discrimination, abuse, and inequality in society. His only mistake was his unconventional approach to explaining himself, which clashed with societal norms.

During that time, Pat encountered the love of his life—a refreshing breeze in the hot, humid summer. She was a black girl, and something about her deeply moved Pat. Before even speaking to her, Pat had already decided he would marry her. There was a spiritual connection, a bond of souls that drew Pat towards BJ.

Before continuing, it's important to introduce BJ, who was remarkably brave and a natural fighter. Her life inspired many girls to assert themselves in the community and advocate for their rights. She was an ideal partner for Pat, and together they reshaped the social fabric in America, particularly in South Bend, Indiana.

"Most women want a man that's already established. A strong woman will be a part of his

struggle, survive it, succeed together, and build an empire.

BJ was the fifth child of Horace Simmons Jr. and Katie Lee Parker. She grew up as a country girl, deeply devoted to her family. Her family meant everything to her, and she cherished them dearly, striving to improve their lives. Her grandfather, Horace Simmons Sr., had seven sons and one daughter, while her father, Horace Simmons Jr., had seven daughters and no sons.

When BJ's father arrived at the hospital, he was denied entry, and only her mother was admitted. BJ has never fully understood why her father brought her mother to the hospital for her birth. It may have been a medical emergency or another urgent reason that compelled her father to take that action.

BJ and her sisters grew up in Monroe County, Forsyth, Georgia, playing along Simmons Road, which still exists today. She was born and raised as a Simmons on Simmons Road.

BJ's birth story is poignant and highlights the racial issues prevalent in America at that time. She was born in **Lamar County, Barnesville, Georgia,** a small town with the nearest hospital to her family's home. Her birth was a response to the pressing health needs her family was confronting at that time.

In December 1954, BJ's father drove her mother to the hospital on a cold day. During this time, racial issues were pervasive in the South, affecting every aspect of life. Hospitals in the area did not admit black people for treatment, forcing black mothers to give birth at home with the help of midwives. BJ's sisters were also born at home under the care of a midwife. It was a time when racism took precedence over human lives, highlighting the stark challenges faced by the black community.

BJ's father, a black man, was not allowed to wait inside the hospital when BJ's mother was admitted. Instead, he was forced to wait outside in his car in the bitterly cold weather, keeping the engine running to stay warm. Exhausted, frustrated, and facing acute discrimination, he eventually fell asleep in the car. While he was sleeping, he accidentally hit the car door knob, fell out, and injured his head, causing bleeding. Now, the hospital had no choice but to treat him, despite their initial reluctance and hesitation due to his race.

At the hospital, BJ's father was asked to write his daughter's name on the birth register. Under immense stress and frustration, he struggled to spell "Barbara." Confused and not fully understanding what he was doing, he made a mistake and wrote "Bobbie Jean" on his daughter's birth certificate instead. For a long time, he believed his daughter's name was Barbara Jean.

BJ's mother had a skin tone that was nearly white, but she was not classified as white. The South had many people like her during that time, reflecting a history of mixed ancestry from earlier eras. She was a diligent woman with a strong drive to improve her family's circumstances and nurture her children into better individuals. Professionally, she worked as a bookkeeper for a white man who owned a large car. She was employed at Pilgrims Life Insurance, where her responsibilities included recording people's names and collecting monthly insurance payments from them. Every morning, BJ's mother dressed impeccably before heading to work, always looking elegant in her dresses. She rode in the back seat of her white employer's large car, traveling across Monroe County and Bibb County to collect payments. Her job required her to visit various areas to fulfill her duties efficiently.

Despite the challenging circumstances for black people in

South, BJ's mother was undeterred. She wasn't afraid to ride in her white employer's car because she was focused on providing for her children. Her job put food on the table, covered educational and household expenses, and she faced criticism from both black and white communities. However, her sense of humor, leadership, and bravery empowered her to ignore negativity. She endured hardships to instill humanity and dedication in her daughters. With only girls in her household, she taught them invaluable lessons about resilience and staying true to their path in life. BJ's mother became a shining example and role model for her daughters.

Whether it was seeing a glimpse of her mother in BJ or her own charisma that caught Pat's attention at first sight, Pat was a strong-willed personality who wasn't easily impressed. However, BJ stood out to him from the moment he saw her. It wasn't her beauty, race, or external qualities that drew him in; rather, it was a spiritual connection that Pat sensed. He made a decisive commitment that she would be his wife. This wasn't just an emotional choice but a declaration driven by the unwavering dedication of a true hero.

On the other hand, BJ hadn't expected to meet anyone from a different race. She wasn't easily impressed by others. She enrolled at **West Georgia College in Carrollton, Georgia**, seeking the college experience and a chance to live independently. She aimed to gain more life experience, make new friends, and discover the deeper meaning of life away from home.

Pat fell in love with BJ during college. He didn't dwell on race, skin color, or negativity; his mind was filled only with love. Tall, charming, and a basketball player, Pat might have been the subject of many girls' dreams, but BJ was the first to capture his heart. He wanted to approach her sincerely, not like a sales pitch. He prayed to God for someone who could understand him and share his burdens. Pat sought a life partner who could offer him pure love and support, having endured criticism and betrayal in the past.

It's often said that when you truly love someone, the universe conspires to bring you together. Pat was trying to find a way to approach BJ when he was pleasantly surprised to find her standing in his room one day. A week or two later, at a college party, Pat saw BJ again. Interestingly, BJ wasn't a basketball fan; she actually loved baseball, especially the Atlanta Braves. What's more, she didn't realize that dating a basketball player was a significant thing.

At the time, most basketball players lived in a dorm known as S-19. During a college party in the dorm, BJ passed by and stopped at Pat's room. Whether it was fate or BJ's curiosity about the albums in Pat's room, they found themselves standing there while everyone else prepared for the party. Pat had nearly 300 albums, sparking BJ's interest and prompting her to strike up a conversation with him about them.

When BJ began talking to Pat, she discovered a well-mannered young man standing before her, who perfectly fit the description of a gentleman her mother had often mentioned. He wasn't flirting or shy, and importantly, he showed no signs of racial bias towards her. Pat was gentle and treated BJ with kindness. Impressed, she wanted to continue talking to this tall guy who was also the town's best basketball player.

They began discussing music, and before long, BJ found herself opening up to Pat about her sister Tina, who had Down Syndrome. She couldn't quite understand why she was sharing such personal details with this young man during their first conversation. Yet, she noticed Pat was actively listening, responding kindly to her questions.

Pat felt incredibly happy that BJ, the love of his life and dream girl, was in his room talking to him and sharing personal details. He made sure to compose himself, avoiding any behavior that might seem flirtatious or overly eager. Instead, he listened attentively to her without making any inappropriate moves like trying to kiss her or putting his arm around her.

BJ was deeply impressed by Pat's respectful behavior, his genuine interest in her, and the way he responded to her questions thoughtfully. They engaged in deep conversations, oblivious to the storm their interracial relationship would soon stir, as such relationships were highly frowned upon during that time.

While they were talking, BJ noticed that it was getting late and time for her to leave. She realized she needed to walk back to her dorm. Another kind gesture from Pat touched her heart deeply: he offered to escort her back to her dorm. This act of chivalry further endeared Pat to BJ, solidifying his place in her heart.

It was a chilly October evening, and as Pat walked BJ back to her dorm, he noticed she was feeling the cold. Without hesitation, he offered her his jacket to shield her from the brisk wind. BJ was touched by Pat's thoughtful gesture, appreciating his caring nature. Unbeknownst to her, Pat was also subtly conveying his affection through his actions. When they reached the entrance of BJ's dorm, she pondered how to return Pat's jacket. Being new to college, she didn't realize that Pat was not just any guy—he was a well-known basketball player, admired by many in the town and at school.

Their first interaction marked the beginning of a lifelong relationship filled with love and understanding. Pat and BJ didn't allow the color of their skin or societal consequences to hinder their connection. They were simply two beautiful souls drawn to each other, eager to explore life together and cherish their love.

Pat was thrilled and eager to share his newfound love with his brother. Excitedly, he announced, ***"Hey, I've got to tell you something—I have a girlfriend!"*** David was genuinely happy for him, knowing Pat needed someone who could love him and understand his thoughts and feelings.

However, David's happiness faded when Pat disclosed that his girlfriend was black. This revelation shocked David; while he didn't hold such biases himself, he understood the potential consequences. Expressing genuine concern, David warned Pat that their parents might not approve. Curious about his brother's perspective, Pat asked David for his opinion. David responded, ***"I love you, Pat. The color of your girlfriend doesn't matter to me."*** His words brought immense relief to Pat, who was grateful that his brother accepted him and understood his feelings.

He was in college, hanging out with BJ and pushing hard to succeed in basketball and make it to the NBA. He had big dreams and the skills to stand out in the NBA. Little did he know that society wouldn't accept his relationship. Black students at his college tried to flirt with his girlfriend, while white teammates complained to the coach that Pat was disrupting the team. His interracial relationship was causing issues, leading to a lack of teamwork.

Pat's coach once told him he could help him join the NBA, but only if he ended things with his girlfriend, whom the coach referred to simply as a "black girl." However, this woman meant everything to Pat. He had planned his future with her, determined to marry her no matter what. Pat believed he could pursue both his basketball career and his relationship with BJ. He never imagined anyone would be so prejudiced as to jeopardize his dreams. Unfortunately, Pat didn't make it to the NBA. Years later, at their 30th reunion, the coach introduced Pat in a way that touched everyone in the audience, numbering between 500 and 600 people. He began, "Before I introduce Pat, *I must apologize to him, his wife, and his daughter. I hurt them deeply, unintentionally. I realize now that what I did was beyond what I understood at the time*." Pat felt a sense of closure that night, forgiving the coach who had once wounded him deeply.

They were dating, and their relationship was well-known on campus, considered unconventional at the time. Pat, a prominent basketball player, was widely recognized. However, BJ's parents were unaware she was seeing a white guy. When her father discovered their relationship, his reaction was humorous. He remarked, "I think that guy must be on drugs, just look at how blue his eyes are."

Pat and BJ faced widespread disapproval of their relationship from his family, teachers, and fellow students at college. They felt isolated amidst a sea of opposition. Eventually, they moved into an apartment off-campus, pooling together the monthly allowances sent by their parents to cover their expenses. They lived as outcasts within the college and beyond.

One day, while shopping for groceries in downtown Carrolton, Pat and BJ noticed a white couple watching them. Unaware that they were being followed, they finished their shopping and prepared to leave the store. The couple's gaze lingered on them, clearly uncomfortable with the sight of a black girl and a white boy together. Pat's height and their distinctive Afros made them stand out wherever they went. The couple's disapproving stares hinted at something amiss in their eyes, as if they perceived something inherently wrong with Pat and BJ.

During a time when Pat and BJ faced intense opposition, it felt as if their relationship was seen as criminal. One night, while Pat was driving with BJ, they were stopped by Georgia State Troopers for running a yellow light at 2 o'clock in the morning. Pat, who was high on Owsley acid or LSD, was behind the wheel. However, the police arrested BJ and took her to the county jail. Her only "crime" was being a black woman traveling with a white man. Confused and frightened, BJ couldn't understand why she was being taken in when she wasn't even driving. They locked her in a cell without processing her entry or taking her fingerprints. The conditions were grim, and BJ feared for her life, questioning the law and what would happen to her. Pat, still a student at the time, had to gather the bond money to secure her release. The jail cell had a dirt floor. BJ's thoughts were I could die in here.

Their families remain unaware of that incident to this day. Pat and BJ endured numerous hardships, and these examples are just a glimpse into their struggles. Recalling these painful memories still evokes strong emotions of anger and sorrow for them. Their journey together has been marked by resilience in the face of adversity.

Chapter 3

Chapter # 3, Something Bigger Than Us

S ometimes, we believe that overcoming our current problem will bring us lasting freedom. In love, we often think that marrying the person we choose is the toughest hurdle, and after that, everything will be smooth. However, life is unpredictable, and we frequently encounter challenges we never anticipated.

At that time, BJ and Pat believed their problems would be resolved once they got married. Pat was confident he could play in the NBA and marry his love. However, they didn't realize that even bigger challenges awaited them. Life had chosen a difficult path for them, one that would make history. They became travelers on challenging roads with no place to rest. In their pursuit of happiness, they were forging a path for themselves, facing obstacles they had never anticipated.

Pat and BJ managed their apartment and expenses through Pat's scholarship money and the monthly allowances sent by their parents. Pat not only knew how to love and protect BJ but also understood the importance of handling their financial responsibilities. He was a true gentleman in every sense.

After finishing school, Pat needed a job to support their household. He felt depressed and frustrated due to the emotional and financial crises they were facing, with no one around to offer support during that difficult time.

In 1975, Pat and BJ returned to his hometown. BJ's father insisted that if she was to live in South Bend, Indiana she had to marry Pat, as he wouldn't allow any of his daughters to live with someone without being married. Pat had no job, no source of income, and no family support. While searching for a job, he met a guy at a party.

The guy was a student from Vermont. Pat was astonished when he said he had heard good things about him and wanted to meet. The student offered to cover Pat's rent until he found a job, asking only that Pat pay him back when he was able. This act of kindness made Pat realize the providence of God.

Pat had some good friends who recognized his kind heart. They understood that, although his views differed from society's norms, he was doing the right thing. Pat didn't want to hurt anyone but aimed to show that all human beings are equal.

His actions weren't driven by a desire for fame or to provoke others; it was his inner voice that refused to let him hate people based on the color of their skin.

Now that Pat and BJ were in South Bend, they needed to obtain a marriage license. They knew it would be difficult for a white man to marry a black woman due to cultural opposition and lack of support. One of Pat's long-time friends, Frankie Anderson, came to their aid. Frankie's mother was a deputy clerk at St. Joseph County Clerk's office and had the courage to help them. She facilitated the process, helping them get their marriage license and blood tests. Without her assistance, they might not have been able to marry. She was a sweet, kind woman with a heart of gold, mediating every matter to ensure their marriage could happen.

Finally, the day came when Pat and BJ were married by the justice of the peace. BJ took a copy of their marriage license and sent it to her father, who had insisted that she could never live with any man without being married.

Though they never hid their marriage, Pat was uncertain about his family's reaction. He knew his parents were good people but also aware of the racial sentiments ingrained in their community. However, their marriage brought unexpected positive changes. Pat's father, initially resistant, gradually softened. Despite having no job or income, Pat's parents began supporting him and BJ. They gave him a car, and his mother started bringing them groceries. Pat's brother David and his sister also began visiting, showing their love for him. This familial support drew the ire of local racists, but Pat's family stood by him, ready to face any challenges out of their love for their "bad boy."

Pat, once a simple and supportive young man, found himself drawn into substance abuse by the pressures of a racist society. With nowhere else to turn, he sought solace in drugs.

His addiction to alcohol and drugs spiraled out of control, deeply upsetting BJ. She wrestled with the painful question of why she had married the man of her dreams, only to watch him lose himself to addiction.

That was their reality in South Bend. They were married, had weathered numerous challenges, and faced an uncertain future. Pat struggled with addiction, leaving BJ to ponder how they could move forward when he wasn't himself. Now, they both had to confront their inner demons and fight their own battles.

Time was about to change, and it needed to. Pat's addiction was holding him back, but as the saying goes, "a man's perspective shifts when he becomes or is about to become a father." Pat's realization came after they found out they were expecting. It was his encounter with Christ—a turning point and a spiritual rebirth. God placed something in his heart that transformed him completely. "There was a train on the tracks; the conductor had clothes on his body but no face. Instead, there was an empty space emitting laughter. I said I would kill you. I was paralyzed by the light from the train's engine. I heard the Lord's voice saying, 'I am letting go of you; you've resisted me long enough.'" It was a moment when Pat was on his knees, crying out to God. This encounter with Christ changed him profoundly. The old addicted Pat was gone, replaced by a new beginning. He discarded his albums, drugs, and everything that had plagued him in the past.

Pat's transformation was complete. He was wholly a new man, known for his commitment to finishing what he started. God impressed upon him that he couldn't forgive himself without forgiving others first. He frequented Shorty Poppas a Black establishment in town engaging people in conversations about life after death. He sought answers, driven by a desire to steer humanity away from racism and destruction.

Pat's rebirth marked a new era of evolution and revolution. He made a solemn vow to assist others facing life's challenges, aiming to shield them from the hardships he himself had endured. His goal was to offer people a meaningful life. It was during this time that Pat conceived the idea of "**_Heroes Camp._**"

One day, BJ and Pat hosted a guest speaker from the Bronx who shared about street ministry and the Yogi Bear Bible study school. He emphasized taking the Gospel to the streets to fulfill their ministry, reaching out to young kids and leading them to Christ. He challenged them, asking if they were afraid to go into the neighborhoods. Pat, however, was fearless in his commitment to ministry. He believed that failing to invite people to church would provoke God's displeasure. The idea of Heroes Camp was already brewing in Pat's heart; he aimed to encourage people to reflect on their lives and cultivate a connection with God and the church. The speaker not only inspired them to call people to church but also empowered the couple to make a significant impact.

Both Pat and BJ were determined to revive the church and share their life lessons with others. This time, they weren't alone. Their daughter Kelly Perri joined them as the third founder of Heroes Camp. She wasn't just a co-founder but a tri-founder of the initiative.

Kelly began serving in the ministry at the young age of seven. She accompanied Pat while he hammered and painted the first gym floor, spreading the messages he wrote on the gym walls. The gym, nearly the size of a basketball court, featured two hoops. She witnessed Pat's struggles with addiction and played a role in his transformation. Kelly painted walls, cleaned up debris, and enthusiastically joined in every activity. She saw firsthand how her father turned a neglected space into a beacon of hope for many.

During the first week, Pat and his daughter took to the streets to spread their message. Pat challenged kids to compete in a game of basketball against him, promising a new pair of sneakers to anyone who could beat him. He was eager to engage kids in a new adventure. Throughout those seven years, Kelly encouraged kids to try and beat her dad for a chance to win new shoes. No one ever beat him.

Everyone thought they could beat that older white man, Pat. But Pat had a deeper lesson to impart through basketball. He sat with them, fostering a caring atmosphere and ministering to their hearts. The camp was centrally located in the heart of South Bend, just a block away from the bus stop, making it accessible to everyone without needing special transportation. Pat spread a message of positivity aimed at liberating people from the mental prisons they had built for themselves. Each weekend, the church would see 50 to 70 bikes and between 55 to 255 individuals attending—a promising start to the journey towards Heroes Camp.

The founders of Heroes Camp held a firm belief that God desired a group of champions akin to David's heroes in the bible. They felt called to mentor young boys without fathers, nurturing them into champions who could serve both God and humanity, making a real impact in the lives of others.

In 1989, a significant transition occurred as Pat and his team moved from the LESEA ministry to New Wings of Faith led by Senior Pastor Willie Coates Jr. Pat served on staff there, and it was during this time that the vision for Heroes Camp began to take shape. Initially renting facilities, they stayed there for six weeks before seeking a larger space to expand their mission. They briefly occupied the Indiana Democratic Club before settling at 2501 Indiana Court for six years. In 2007, they acquired their current base at 4130 Hickory Road, which Pat particularly liked for its gym with a wooden floor. They considered another property until a fellow believer felt led to build a gym specifically for Pat due to the large number of local children involved. Soon after, the owner of the Hickory Road gym contacted Pat, offering to sell the property. After evaluating the location, Pastor Coates and Pat prayed together in the movies 14-parking lot, listened to music, and received affirmation to proceed. They acquired the building for $1.2 million, securing the future of Heroes Camp.

Brandon McKnight's journey through Heroes Camp illustrates how it provided more than just basketball training—it offered a refuge and a transformative environment for young people like him. Raised in South Bend Indiana, Brandon's introduction to Heroes Camp at the age of seven coincided with his passion for basketball, which was central to his early life. At La Salle High School, where Pat and David also attended, Brandon found a sense of community and purpose through his involvement with the camp. One of Brandon's closest relationships at the camp was with a friend who played a significant role in his basketball rituals, such as cutting his hair before each game. This bond was pivotal for Brandon, but it was shattered when his friend and the friend's brother and nephew were involved in a tragic incident—an event that deeply affected Brandon and made him confront the potential dangers he might have faced if circumstances had been different. Brandon attributes his safety and resilience during such challenging times to the prayers and support of his family, as well as the nurturing environment provided by Heroes Camp. He acknowledges that his connection with the camp was a lifeline that steered him away from potential pitfalls and helped him grow into a better person both on and off the basketball court. Through his experiences at **Heroes Camp,** Brandon came to appreciate the profound blessing of God in his life. The camp not only sharpened his basketball skills but also shielded him from the harsh realities of life, offering him guidance, mentorship, and a strong sense of community. His story underscores the vital role that Heroes Camp plays in shaping the lives of young individuals, providing them with the tools and support needed to navigate challenges and thrive.

They began integrating teachings of the Lord into their home, aiming to empower fatherless children as champions of God. Starting with humble beginnings, they maintained their momentum to support as many kids as possible at Heroes Camp. From day one, the Camp was filled with children of various ages. Pat initiated Bible sessions alongside the three classes, optional for those interested in hearing God's word. BJ has overseen the dining table since the Camp's inception, baking cookies and lasagna for the kids while also teaching them Bible lessons. The Camp served not only as a training ground but also as a home for the Magley family and numerous homeless, parentless, and troubled children. Nearly 30 different individuals have lived with them since the Camp began. In exchange for their stay, they are asked to share the Gospel.

Heroes Camp meant more to David than just playing

basketball; it was where he found the best players. One day, a troubled young man, who had been in trouble and even jailed at just 12 years old, joined the Camp. He was tough and had a rough past. After a session, while walking home with Pat, David questioned why Pat allowed this guy into the Camp. Pat explained that he didn't pray to God only for the best; he prayed for those who were in need. If they didn't help him, who would? This revelation shocked David. He realized that Heroes Camp was not just about basketball; it was about saving souls. It was about fulfilling the mission that Pat believed God had given him.

Garry McCallum, a senior pastoral staff member at Heroes Camp, first heard about the Camp in 1993 while visiting South Bend with a friend. They were attending a church affiliated with New Wings of Faith, where they discovered the Camp's gym behind the sanctuary. Intrigued, Garry learned about Pat Magley and the work of Heroes Camp. Garry eventually moved to Indiana in 2000 and formally connected with Heroes Camp in 2003. By 2004, he began volunteering there. It was Pat Magley's love, dedication, and determination that deeply resonated with Garry, inspiring him to get involved.

Jaraan Cornell, the program coordinator at Heroes Camp, was born and raised in South Bend, Indiana. He first encountered Pat when he was 13 years old, through friends who had already met him. One Saturday morning, while looking for a place to play basketball, his friends introduced him to Pat at Madison Recreation. Pat challenged Jaraan: if he could beat him, he'd earn a new pair of shoes. Jaraan was confident no white boy could outplay him, but the next week, Pat defeated him 21-0. Disappointed yet inspired, Jaraan began training under Pat, which ultimately led to a full scholarship to a Division One university. Now, having earned his degree, Jaraan serves at Heroes Camp, passing on what he learned there. He's dedicated to realizing Pat's vision: encouraging people to remember their past, learn from it, and empower others to change their futures.

Dr. Mario and Regina Villela, founders of Servants of the Street Ministry in Elkhart, Indiana, both had tumultuous pasts marked by addiction, jail time, and rehabilitation centers. Their lives were transformed by God, prompting them to dedicate themselves to serving Him. They moved to Indiana from San Antonio, Texas, in 1995 as an interracial couple seeking a supportive faith community. Through connections, they met Apostle Willie Coates and discovered New Wings of Faith, where they also met Pat Magley. Since then, they've maintained a strong connection with him and Heroes Camp. Dr. Mario began volunteering at Heroes Camp, providing cooking services. Concurrently, they run a recovery ministry called Boot Camp, a rigorous spiritual program where participants were confined for 90 days. Witnessing Pat's dedication to calling people to God, training them in basketball, and fostering personal growth deeply impressed them.

Noe Cabello, a friend of Pat Magley, originally from Texas, moved to Indiana due to his father's involvement with a ministry. He met Pat nearly 30 years ago, and their friendship was not merely a coincidence but felt ordained by God. They bonded over their mutual love for tennis. Pat, always athletic, continually sought new avenues to showcase his talents. Noe witnessed and vividly remembers the inception, evolution, and final location of Heroes Camp over the years.

Since its inception, Heroes Camp has been dedicated to helping and educating homeless, fatherless children and at-risk youth, stepping into the parental role and imparting valuable life lessons. Pat Magley has taken on this responsibility with unwavering dedication, fulfilling his duty to these children with compassion and commitment.

. . .

Chapter 4

Push Back to Move Forward

Have you ever watched long-jump athletes? If so, you've probably noticed how they run a few yards before making their leap. You might also have observed tigers hunting. Before pouncing on their prey, tigers step back to focus before moving forward. This concept applies to our lives too. To succeed, we should reflect on our past experiences and use them to propel ourselves forward.

Building the road to Heroes Camp was tough, but the most challenging part was rescuing kids from the streets and giving them a new life. Pat, BJ, and their daughter Kelly not only paved that road but also transformed many lives. For 25 years, Heroes Camp has been active in Mishawaka, dedicated to bringing every child off the streets and into basketball. They've impacted nearly 75,000 people, overcoming setbacks, storms, and obstacles along the way. While Pat may never play in the NBA himself, he's trained countless others to achieve their dreams. What was once an outlaw is now a guiding light for many. Despite their age, Pat and BJ continue tirelessly caring for parentless children, while Kelly pursues her father's vision with unwavering dedication.

Spirituality and God's love still illuminate Pat's heart. Whether rain or shine, sickness or fatigue, one can often find him deep in prayer, alone or with others. It was through Pat's prayers that Heroes Camp was saved from complete collapse.

On July 1, 2014, around 11 tornadoes touched down in Michiana during a devastating storm. Surveillance video from Heroes Camp captured an actual vortex passing through the building. Garry McCallum received a call from the alarm company at four in the morning, alerting him to the alarm. He rushed to the Camp and found widespread destruction. Trees were uprooted, and darkness enveloped the area. As he approached, he noticed the roof being peeled off, struggling to believe what he saw, wondering if he might be dreaming. Garry called Pat and urged him to come immediately. When Pat arrived and opened the door, a mix of anger and fear washed over him as he confronted the devastation before him.

P.J. Perri, son-in-law and Director of Operations and Development at Heroes Camp, initially served one day a week but soon became captivated by Pat and BJ Magley's vision. Eventually, he left his job to fully dedicate himself to the ministry. He served as a pastor, minister, and youth director, contributing across all areas of the Camp. He, also married Kelly the daughter of Pat/BJ. The July 2014 storm was a pivotal moment for him and his role at Heroes Camp. As the tornado approached, P.J. was preparing for the arrival of his new baby. When his wife Kelly asked about his early morning plans, he explained the storm situation. The news shocked her, evoking a flood of emotions as she imagined the scene outside. The Camp was gripped by grief, shock, anger, sadness, and stress in the aftermath of the storm.

The roof and north wall of the Camp were destroyed, leaving Pat devastated, fearing the children had lost their home. It was heartbreaking for both Pat and BJ, who had invested every penny into Heroes Camp. They faced uncertainty about how to handle the situation and repair the damage. It seemed like Heroes Camp might not recover. The storm had chosen to challenge Pat and BJ's patience and dedication to their mission.

Despite the storm demolishing the Heroes Camp building, it couldn't crush the heroism within Pat. After a group prayer, Pat pondered and sought a new place for the children. Despite losing everything, he remained determined to find another building for them. Pat had successfully planted the seed of Heroes Camp in people's hearts, and now it was time to reignite their faith and passion. Within a week, after scouting several locations, they settled on a new building and swiftly relocated the children. Pat prayed fervently and committed himself to rebuilding. This time, he wasn't alone; a dedicated team of pastors, teachers, and administrators at the Camp worked tirelessly day and night. They took on roles as plumbers, masons, and carpenters to construct wooden roofs and walls for the Camp. However, they faced challenges from the insurance company, which refused to cover the storm damage costs.

The destruction of the Camp displaced its owners and kids, leading many to believe restarting in the same location was impossible. However, Pat and BJ believed that God had chosen that place for the fatherless children and future heroes. Despite being out of the building for 15 months, they continued training, teaching, and supporting the kids at various locations. The Camp remained operational but scattered. After 15 months, they returned to their original home. The heroes were reunited at their Camp, guided by their life hero, Mr. Pat.

Chapter 5

Chapter #5, Faith Restored

At some point in our lives, many of us face the need for a rebirth or a transformative change to live the life we desire. Some people are fortunate to experience revolutionary and evolutionary processes effortlessly. However, others must navigate a challenging path to transform their lives.

The tornado that struck Heroes Camp was more than just a storm; it was a profound test of faith and beliefs for everyone there. Many doubted their ability to survive such devastation, considering the Camp's size and the high repair costs. Yet, the resilient old man had the fortitude to face any storm life threw at him. He steadfastly believed that God would provide miraculous help in their time of need.

After 15 to 16 months, when Heroes Camp reopened its gates to the children, it was a moment of immense joy and happiness for everyone involved. The Camp embraced them like a loving mother welcoming her children home. The place that had been destroyed just a year ago was now restored and fully operational. Through its actions, the Camp conveyed a powerful message: while bad things happen, they do not define your entire life. It showed that good can be extracted from challenging situations. Pat and his team at the Camp exemplified real-life heroes who courageously dedicated themselves to the ministry and to caring for children.

The mega relaunch party of Heroes Camp was monumental. It symbolized the Camp's return to the spotlight, marking the end of tough times and the restoration aided by God. They distributed 1000 t-shirts bearing the message **"knocked down, but not out,"** reflecting their resilient spirit. The event drew a large crowd, filled with happiness and celebration. It felt like a rebirth for the Camp, featuring new colors, walls, floors, and a roof. Additional facilities were introduced, providing a fresh start for the Camp's heroes who rediscovered motivation and renewed faith in themselves. Through their trial, the Camp and its heroes persevered, and with God's grace, they were back in their original building.

For 35 years, Heroes Camp has been dedicated to rescuing children from the streets, guiding them on the basketball court, and illuminating their path with knowledge and self-empowerment. A cherished addition to the Camp, close to BJ's heart, is Katie P. Simmons Kitchen Dining Commons, which can now serve 100 campers at once. The old one could only serve 18 campers at one sitting. Despite this, the Saturday sessions brought nearly 100 children to the Camp, prompting someone to suggest expanding the kitchen. Initially hesitant due to past challenges, BJ found herself reluctant to entertain the idea. Yet, as always, the Camp and its founder felt the guiding hand of God. With divine assistance, BJ's vision for expanding the kitchen to accommodate 100 seats and a state-of-the-art facility became a reality, beautifully enhancing the Camp's capabilities.

Truly, it was a divine blessing that a facility completely devastated by the storm not only resumed functioning but also expanded. Today, the Camp boasts a spacious waiting area, a large dining hall, an exceptional kitchen, a weight room, clothing or gear shop, barbershop and a recording studio—all provided free of charge to the children and young men. Since its inception, the Camp has remained steadfast in its mission: ensuring no child ends up on the streets due to lack of resources or parental support. At Heroes Camp, the staff—comprising parents, teachers, and ministers—nurture and mentor these children, molding them into future heroes without any financial burden. This commitment has been unwavering since day one, dedicated to empowering and uplifting every child who walks through their doors.

During the restoration, it was more than just rebuilding the physical structure; it was about restoring faith. The relaunch ceremony attracted numerous influential figures from the business world and the local community. Representatives from brands like Nike visited Heroes Camp and generously donated to support the children. These visitors witnessed firsthand the transformative impact of Pat, BJ, Kelly, PJ (Patrick Perri) the dedicated staff at Heroes Camp. They saw how lives were being changed, not just within the Camp but throughout South Bend. By nurturing and mentoring children, they are cultivating future contributors to the community, making a meaningful and lasting difference.

Now Pat reflects on his early memories, finding meaning in Dr. King's death and seeing it as not in vain but as the fruit of his labor. He believes he may not be a role model in the traditional sense, but he is reliable in his commitment. Through his ministry and the work at Heroes Camp, he is steadfast in his mission to combat racial discrimination and uplift children. At Heroes Camp, not every child dreams of becoming an NBA player; some aspire to be teachers, accountants, or pursue other paths. The Camp provides comprehensive support—physical, emotional, spiritual, and financial—to help these children thrive and achieve their aspirations in life. It stands as a reliable beacon of hope and transformation for the youth it serves.

The impact of Heroes Camp's teachings may not manifest overnight. The children arrive at the Camp from diverse backgrounds and at various stages of their lives, having endured significant challenges such as difficult family situations, lack of parental care, and various social and mental issues. At Heroes Camp, these children undergo a healing and transformation process. They are nurtured into stronger individuals, equipped with skills to become self-sufficient, pursue careers of their choice, and contribute positively to society. The Camp plays a crucial role in guiding them towards independence and a fulfilling future.

The heroes of Heroes Camp generously offer free facilities to every child, supported by donations to cover the Camp's expenses. The Magley family has dedicated their lives to the well-being of these children and to their ministry. The Camp actively collects donations through both online platforms and physical resources. For those who prefer online donations, they can visit the Heroes Camp website, where verification and secure transactions are ensured. Additionally, local community members, banks, and organizations are encouraged to visit the Camp in person to witness its impact firsthand and make informed decisions about supporting its mission.

If you're considering donating to Heroes Camp, remember that every penny you contribute makes a meaningful impact. It's not just an emotional decision influenced by the Camp's compelling story; rather, it's a call from your spirit to potentially change a child's life by supporting their yearly expenses. Donors who have visited the Camp after making multiple contributions have been amazed by the tangible results of their support. If you have the compassion and willingness to make a difference in the lives of homeless and parentless children, consider donating. It's a chance to receive God's blessing by contributing to a greater cause that enriches and transforms young lives.

In the words of Sammy Brown, a former teammate and longtime friend of Pat, "Pat is like a father and a mother to these kids. His impact is widely recognized, both among those he helps directly and throughout the community at **Heroes Camp.**"

According to Jan Fye, a longtime friend of Pat and BJ, she recalls the day she first met the couple. It was back in 1974 when they were all living in the same building. Jan was intrigued as it was her first encounter with an interracial couple. She was impressed by Pat and BJ and admired their efforts.

According to Herman Smith, a longtime friend of Pat, *"he loved witnessing the progress of Heroes Camp, and he often tells people that the first thing they experience at the Camp is love."*

Life at Heroes Camp is not just a story; it's a profound experience. Regardless of their age, every child is warmly welcomed, loved, and receives proper education at the Camp. Pat and BJ Magley, the heroes of the Camp, have achieved what many might hesitate to even consider in their lives.

For 35 years, Heroes Camp has quietly been one of the world's best-kept historical secrets. Its heroes have been tirelessly serving the community, though their story has remained largely unknown to many. Now is the time to share their message: life is not defined by challenges alone. You can overcome difficult situations, thrive, and become a significant contributor to your community. Don't let tough circumstances dictate the course of your life. Let the inspiring story of Pat and BJ Magley inspire you to become the best version of yourself. Their journey can show you that with perseverance and faith, you can achieve greatness and make a meaningful impact on the world around you.

For donations and more information about Heroes Camp go to their website, www.heroescamp.com and stay tuned for the documentary, Road to Heroes Camp

Afterword

Life is fleeting, and often, we spend too much time worrying about situations that may never occur. Life isn't always easy; it requires facing challenges to achieve your goals and make your dreams a reality.

Once, life was tough for Pat and BJ. Their only "mistake" was falling in love with each other. They didn't anticipate that the color of their skin would become a significant barrier. Their community refused to accept their relationship, and they faced abandonment from society. Despite the series of challenges they encountered, their faith in themselves and their love for each other remained steadfast. The Magley's have been married now for 49 years and when he looks at her, it's the same look he has when he first met her while in college.

God showed Pat the enlightenment of church and Christ, which helped him emerge from grief and led him to serve in the ministry. This spiritual awakening also aided him in overcoming smoking addiction and forgiving those who had made his life difficult. Despite his dream of playing in the NBA being shattered by racism, Pat found the strength to forgive them, guided by his faith in God. He became an ordained minister in 1989.

While following the path God had laid out for him, Pat conceived the idea of Heroes Camp—a place where homeless and parentless children could be nurtured and educated. With the support of his wife BJ and daughter Kelly, he embarked on this mission despite facing numerous obstacles, including a devastating tornado that destroyed the Heroes Camp. Despite lacking funds and resources, their unwavering faith in God sustained them, driving them to rebuild the facility and provide a home for these children once more.

Pat, BJ, Kelly, and all the members of the Camp dedicated their lives to a cause greater than themselves. Their commitment surpassed personal dreams and aspirations—they became true heroes, paving the way for many others. Their selfless service to humanity and their visionary ideals will resonate through history. They have left an indelible mark, shaping a legacy that will endure far into the future.

Author's Note

Thank you for taking the journey through this story. It was a labor of love, and I hope it resonated with you in some way.